Y0-BMG-814

Amazing Love

AN EASTER CELEBRATION OF HOPE

CREATED BY TOM FETTKE

Copyright © 1992 by Pilot Point Music.
All rights reserved.   Litho in U.S.A.

KANSAS CITY, MO 64141

CONTENTS

THE LOVE OF GOD—An Amazing Love 4
    And Can It Be?
    The Love of God

O What Love 14

For God So Loved 19

Because He Loved Us 29

He Takes Away the Sins of the World 31

Rejoice in His Love 40
    My Savior's Love
    Such Love

And Can It Be? 49

Lamb of God 51

LIVING HOPE—A Celebration of His Resurrection 57
    Christ Is Alive! Let All Christians Sing
    He Rose
    Jesus Christ Is Alive

My God, I Love You 75

When Praise Demands a Sacrifice 77

HIGH AND EXALTED—Moments of Praise 87
    The Love of God
    Exalt His Name Together
    He Is the Amen

The Love of God
An Amazing Love

Arr. by Tom Fettke

Majestic ♩ = ca. 88

(Charles Wesley - Thomas Campbell)

A little slower ♩ = ca. 84

Arr. © 1992 by Pilot Point Music. All rights reserved.
Administered by Integrated Copyright Group, Inc., P. O. Box 24149, Nashville, TN 37202.

* Copyright 1917. Renewed 1945 and arr. © 1992 by Nazarene Publishing House. All rights reserved.
Administered by Integrated Copyright Group, Inc., P.O. Box 24149, Nashville, TN 37202.

Oh, What Love

TOM FETTKE

FOLK MELODY
Arr. by Tom Fettke

Narrator 1:
The greatest evidence of God's love for us is this: that while we were sinners Christ died for us. Nothing that we have ever done and nothing

that we are doing now ... nothing that we can ever do will merit this love. It cannot be earned and it

cannot be bought ... *(1 John 4:10, Phillips)* **Narrator 2:** Father, thank You for Your amazing love.

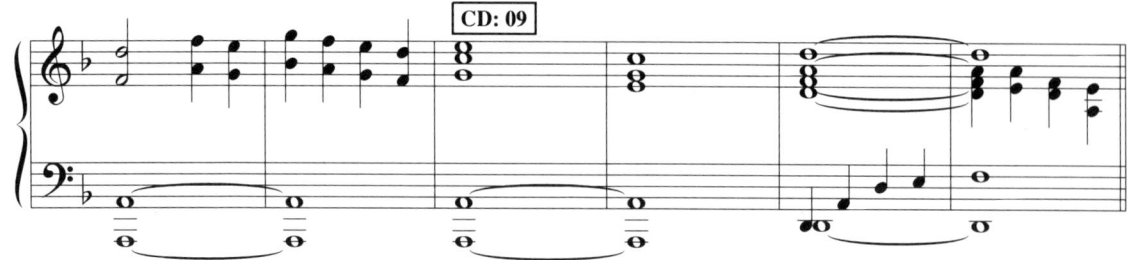

*May be directed in 2 beats per measure to achieve proper nuance.

© 1992 by Pilot Point Music. All rights reserved.
Administered by Integrated Copyright Group, Inc., P.O. Box 24149, Nashville, TN 37202.

*Divide choir equally mixing male and female singers on each of the 4 parts. (You may divide by assigning a part to each of the sections in your SATB choir. However, this is less desirable than mixing male and female on each part.)

For God So Loved

Adapted from Scripture by S. D.

STUART DAUERMANN
Arr. by Tom Fettke

© 1972 by Lillenas Publishing Co. All rights reserved.
Administered by Integrated Copyright Group, Inc., P.O. Box 24149, Nashville, TN 37202.

*Option: duet may be sung by the choir– ladies' and men's parts in unison.

Because He Loved Us

TOM FETTKE

Expressively ♩ = ca. 60

(Start narration at measure 5)

Narrator 1: He was despised and rejected by men, a man of sorrows, and familiar with suffering

Narrator 2: Because he loved us.

Narrator 1: Surely he took our infirmities and carried our sorrows

Narrator 2: Because he loved us.

Narrator 1: He was pierced for our transgressions, he was crushed for our iniquities

Narrator 2: Because he loved us.

Narrator 1: The punishment that brought us peace was upon him, and by his wounds we are healed

Narrator 2: Because he loved us.

Narrator 1: We all, like sheep, have gone astray . . . But the Lord has laid on Jesus the iniquity of us all

Narrator 2: Because God loved us.

Narration based on selected verses from Isaiah 53 (NIV)

© 1992 by Pilot Point Music. All rights reserved.
Administered by Integrated Copyright Group, Inc., P.O. Box 24149, Nashville, TN 37202.

30

Segue to "He Takes Away the Sins of the World"

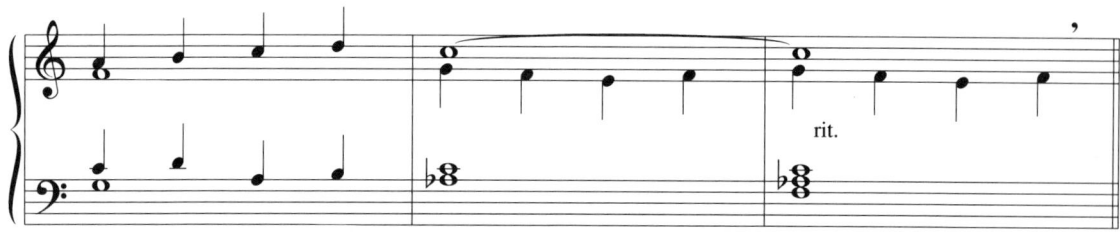

He Takes Away the Sins of the World

KEN BIBLE and PHILIP P. BLISS

PHILIP P. BLISS and TOM FETTKE
Arr. by Tom Fettke

© 1992 by Pilot Point Music. All rights reserved.
Administered by Integrated Copyright Group, Inc., P.O. Box 24149, Nashville, TN 37202.

37

slight rit.   *Solo I*   (53) a tempo
sub. *mp*

Can it be? He takes a-way the sins of the

cresc. poco a poco   **CD: 18**

world.

accel.

Faster ♩ = ca. 76
(58) *Choir*
f

When He comes, our glo-rious King, All His ran-somed

62
cresc.
home to bring. Then a - new this song we'll sing, "Hal - le -
cresc.
62
cresc.
ff
(,)
66
rit. poco a poco
lu - jah! Hal - le - lu - jah! Hal - le - lu - jah!
ff
(,)
66
ff
rit. poco a poco
decresc. poco a poco
What a Sav - ior!"
decresc. poco a poco

39

Choir (or Solo I) **Slower** ♩ = ca. 60

He takes a-way, Je-sus takes a-way, He takes a-way the sins of the world.

Rejoice in His Love

Arr. by Tom Fettke

Narrator: *(Start without music)*
To him who loves us, and has freed us from our sins by his blood *(start music)* and has made us kings and priests to serve God the Father [and rejoice in his love]; to him be glory and power for ever and ever! *(Rev. 1:5b-6, NIV, alt.)*

CD: 19 Tenderly ♩ = ca. 69

"**My Savior's Love**" *(Charles H. Gabriel - C.H.G. and Tom Fettke)*

Ladies unison — Freely

I stand a-mazed in the pres-ence Of Je-sus the Naz-a-rene, And won-der how He could

© 1992 by Pilot Point Music. All rights reserved.
Administered by Integrated Copyright Group, Inc., P.O. Box 24149, Nashville, TN 37202.

love me, A sinner, condemned, unclean.

In tempo ♩ = ca. 69
Choir unison

Oh, how marvelous! How wonderful! And my song shall ever be: Oh, how marvelous! How wonderful! Is my Savior's love for me! He

(Tune by Tom Fettke)

took my sins and my sor - rows, He made them His ver - y own; He bore the bur - dens to Cal - va - ry And suf - fered and died a - lone.

More rhythmic
(Soloist may continue through measure 41)
32
mf
Oh, how mar-vel-ous! How won-der-ful! And my song shall
Ab Bbm7 Cm7 Fm7 Bbm7
36
ev - er be: Oh, how mar-vel-ous! How won-der-ful!
Db/Eb Eb7 Ab Bbm7 Cm7 Fm7
CD: 22
rit. and dim.
On 3rd beat-
New tempo starts ♩ = 116
Is my Sav - ior's love for me, for me!
me!
Bbm Ab/C Db6 Ab/Eb Eb7 Db/Ab Eb/Ab Db/Ab Ab
rit. and dim.

44

*"My Savior's Love" *(Charles H. Gabriel)*

Such love, such wondrous love! Such love, such wondrous love! That God should love a sinner such as I, How wonderful is love like this!

*© 1929, Renewed 1957 and arr. © 1992 by Lillenas Publishing Co. All rights reserved.
Administered by Integrated Copyright Group, Inc., P.O. Box 24149, Nashville, TN 37202.

Brighter and stronger

Oh, how mar-vel-ous! How won-der-ful! And my song shall ev-er be: Oh, how mar-vel-ous! How won-der-ful! Is my Sav-ior's love for me!

CD: 24

Solo or 1st sopranos **ff**

Such

love! _____ Such

Oh, how mar-vel-ous! How won-der-ful! And my song shall ev-er be:

love! _____ His love! ___

Oh, how mar-vel-ous! How won-der-ful! Is my Sav-ior's love,

76
His love!
Is my Savior's love,
Is my Savior's love
76
Cm7
B♭/D
E♭6
B♭/F
80
For me!
for me!
80
Fsus
F
B♭

And Can It Be?

CHARLES WESLEY

THOMAS CAMPBELL
Arr. by Tom Fettke

can it be That Thou, my God, shouldst die for me?

Segue to "Lamb of God"

Lamb of God

T. P.

TWILA PARIS
Arr. by Tom Fettke

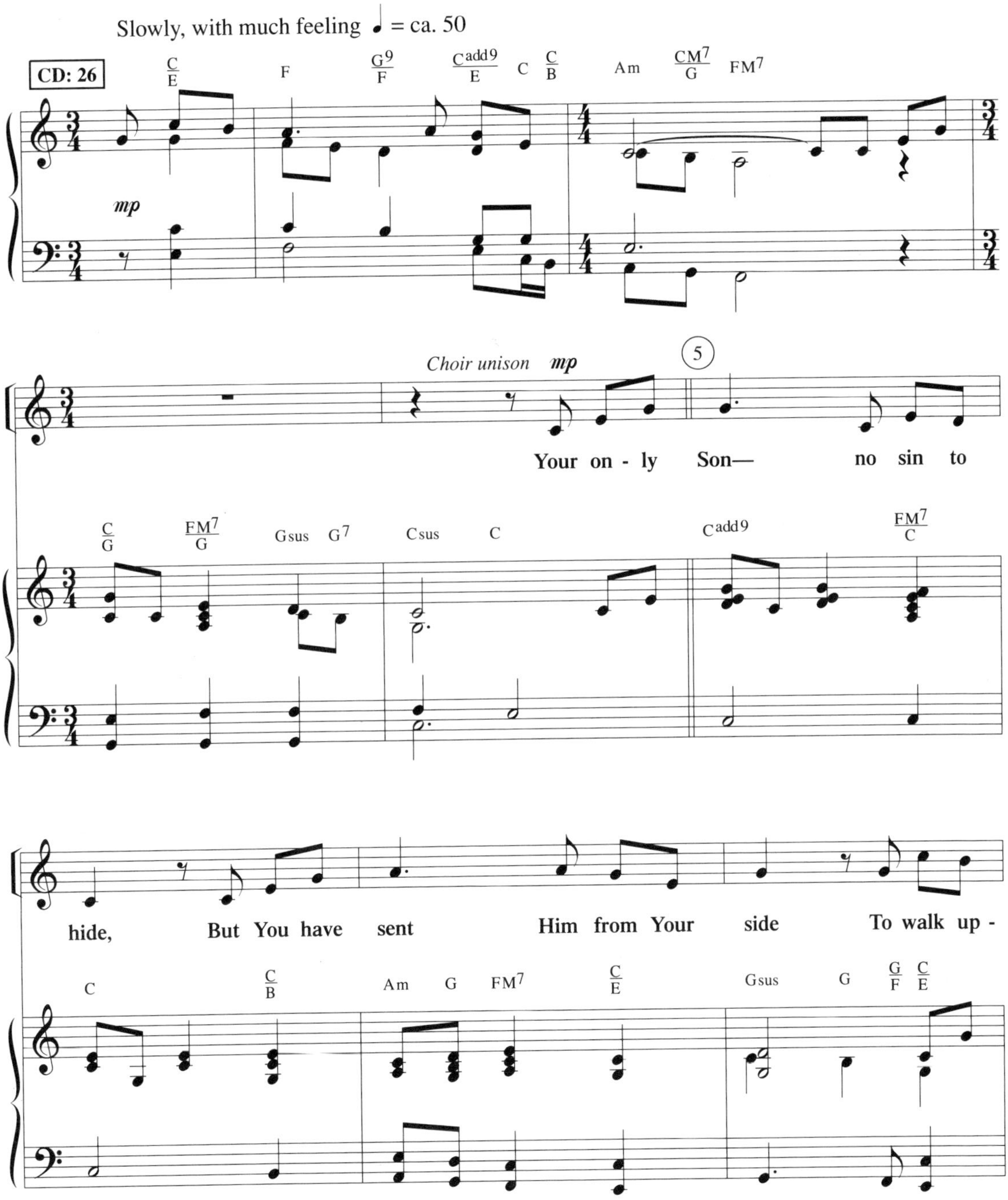

on this guilt-y sod and to be-come the Lamb of God. Your gift of Love they cru-ci-fied; They laughed and scorned Him as He died. The hum-ble King they named a fraud And sac-ri-ficed the Lamb of

53

God. O Lamb of God, sweet Lamb of God, I love the ho-ly Lamb of God. Oh, wash me in His pre-cious blood, My Jesus Christ, the Lamb of God.

I was so lost_____ I should have died, But You have brought_____ me to Your side To be led by_____ Your staff and rod, And to be called a lamb of God. O Lamb of God, sweet Lamb of God, I love the ho-ly Lamb of God. Oh, wash me in His pre-cious blood, 'Til I am

cresc.
just a lamb of God. Oh, wash me
f
D♭/F D♭/A♭ A♭sus A♭7 D♭ D♭/F
50
decresc.
in His pre - cious blood, My Je - sus
B♭m B♭m7/A♭ G♭M7 A♭9/G♭ D♭/F D♭ D♭/C B♭m B♭m7/A♭ G♭M7
rit.
mp
God.
(7)
Christ, the Lamb of God, Lamb of God.
God.
D♭/F G♭M7 A♭ D♭ D♭M7 G♭/D♭ D♭

Living Hope
A Celebration of His Resurrection

Arr. by Tom Fettke

(start without music)
Narrator:
We give praise to the *(start music)* God and Father of our Lord Jesus Christ!
In his great mercy he has given us new birth into a living hope through the resurrection of
Jesus Christ from the dead. *(1 Peter 1:3, NIV)*

---

* Measures 6 through 13 include portions of "Christ Arose" by Robert Lowery and "Christ the Lord Is Risen Today" from Lyra Davidica

© 1992 by Pilot Point Music. All rights reserved.
Administered by Integrated Copyright Group, Inc., P.O. Box 24149, Nashville, TN 37202.

58

*"**Christ Is Alive! Let All Christians Sing**" *(Tom Fettke)*

Lyrics: Christ is a-live! Let all Chris-tians sing. Pro-claim His glo-ry to the skies. The First and Last, the liv-ing Lord Brings

*© 1984 by Pilot Point Music. All rights reserved. Administered by Integrated Copyright Group, Inc., P. O. Box 24149, Nashville, TN 37202.

hope of peace for - ev - er-more. Be - cause He rose, we too shall rise. Je - sus, Christ Je - sus is a - live.

Narrator:
"I am the Living One; I was dead, and behold I am alive for ever and ever!

"Christ Arose" *(Robert Lowery)*

㉝ In tempo ♩ = ca. 88

And I hold the keys of death and hell." *(Rev. 1:17-18, NIV)*

cresc.　　　　rit.

New tempo ♩ = ca. 112

㊴ CD: 33

E♭add9

mf

*****"He Rose"** *(Traditional Spiritual and Tom Fettke)*

㊸ Unison *mf*

1. They cru-ci-fied my Sav-ior and nailed Him to the tree, They

Unison *mf*

㊸

N.C.

*©1992 by Pilot Point Music. All rights reserved. Administered by Integrated Copyright Group, Inc., P. O. Box 24149, Nashville, TN 37202.

cru - ci - fied my Sav - ior and nailed Him to the tree, _____ They cru - ci - fied my Sav - ior and nailed Him to the tree, _____ But the Lord a - rose and lives in me. He

rose, He rose, He rose up from the dead! He rose, He rose, He
He rose, He rose, He rose up from the dead! He rose, He rose, He

rose up from the dead! He rose, He rose, He
rose up from the dead! He rose, He rose, He

rose up from the dead! The might-y Lord a-rose and

lives in me.　　　　　　　　　　　　　　　　　　　2. Then

Jo-seph begged His bod-y and laid Him in the tomb, Then

Jo-seph begged His bod-y and laid Him in the tomb, Then

64

Jo-seph begged His bod-y and laid Him in the tomb, But the Lord a-rose and lives in me. He rose, He rose, He rose up from the dead! He rose, He rose, He

He rose, He rose, He rose up from the dead! He rose, He rose, He

65

Mar-y she came run-ning, a-look-ing for my Lord, And
Mar-y she came run-ning, a-look-ing for my Lord, And
Mar-y she came run-ning, a-look-ing for my Lord, But the

Lord a-rose and lives in me. 4. An

an-gel came from heav-en and rolled the stone a-way, An

an-gel came from heav-en and rolled the stone a-way, An

an - gel came from heav - en and rolled the stone a - way,___ And the Lord a-rose and lives in me. He

rose, He rose, He rose up from the dead! He
Unison He rose, He rose, He rose up from the dead!

rose, He rose, He rose up from the dead! He
He rose, He rose, He rose up from the dead!

103
rose, He rose, He rose up from the dead! The might-y
He rose, He rose, He rose up from the dead, The might-y

Lord a-rose and lives in me. The might-y

70

accel. poco a poco   *f*   cresc.

Lord a-rose, the Lord a-rose; The might-y Lord a-rose and

Faster ♩ = ca. 128

lives in me.

CD: 38

*"Jesus Christ Is Alive" *(Jack Hayford)*

131
CD: 39
cause He's a - live I can sing. For
131
A♭ E♭/G B♭/D Cm7 B♭/D E♭(no 3rd) E♭/G
135
death could not o - ver - whelm Him and it can't con - quer
135
A♭ E♭/G E♭ B♭/D Cm7 B♭7/D
139
cresc.
me; And the pow - er of sin is bro - ken And the
cresc.
E♭ E♭/G
139
A♭ E♭/G Cm7
cresc.

73

more. Jesus is alive forever-more. Alleluia! Alleluia!

My God, I Love You

TOM FETTKE

(Start narration at measure 5)

Narrator:

My God, I love You; not because I hope for a place in Your heavenly kingdom; and not fearing that If I don't love You, I might forever die; but because You embraced me and all mankind upon the cross.

For us You bore the nails and spear and public disgrace. You had to endure numberless griefs and torments and bitter agony . . . and death itself . . . and all this for man, who regarded You as an enemy.

Then why, O Savior, should I not love You as well? Not for the sake of winning heaven, or because I fear hell; not with the hope of gaining earthly status or receiving a reward. But as You have loved me, my Lord, even so I love You and I will live in sacrificial praise, even if devotion should cost me everything, solely because You are my God and my Eternal King.

– Tom Fettke, based on a 17th century Latin text

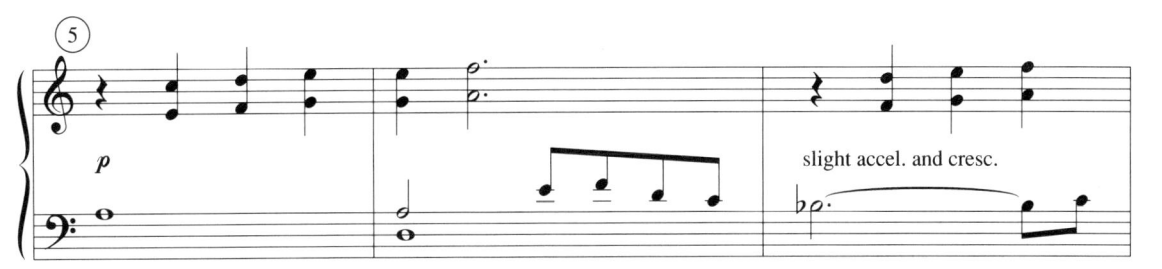

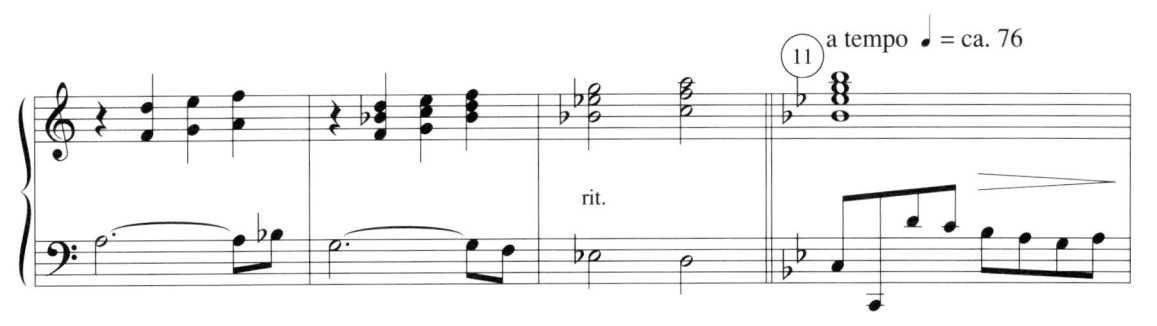

© 1992 by Pilot Point Music. All rights reserved.
Administered by Integrated Copyright Group, Inc., P.O. Box 24149, Nashville, TN 37202.

Segue to "When Praise Demands a Sacrifice"

When Praise Demands a Sacrifice

S. C. S. and R. M.

SUE C. SMITH and RUSSELL MAULDIN
Arr. by Tom Fettke

© 1990 by John T. Benson Co., ASCAP. All rights reserved.
Used by permission of Benson Music Group, Inc.

fore the Lord was not a lamb. He bound his on-ly son, and as the knife was raised, A sac-ri-fice be-came the price of praise. When praise de-

Ladies unison *mf* Stronger *Solo may continue**

Men unison *mf*

cresc.

* If range is not prohibitive, sing melody through measure 38.

mands a sac-ri-fice, I'll wor-ship e-ven then, Sur-
Stronger
ren-der-ing the dear-est things in life. And if de-
And if de-
vo-tion costs me all, He'll find me faith-ful to His call, When

35
praise de - mands a sac - ri - fice.
B♭m7 D♭M7/B♭ B♭m7/E♭ E♭7 D♭/E♭ A♭ A♭/C
39
CD: 44
rit.
Unison
The call to
A add9/C♯ A/C♯ Bm7 D/E E D/E
rit.
42
a tempo
go to Cal - va - ry had come to God's own Son; Where an
Oo God's Son.
Unison
A add9 E/G♯ C♯/E♯ F♯m11 F♯m7 F♯m9 F♯m7
a tempo

al - tar wait - ed for the Lamb He would be - come. His
Oo would be - come. His

hands reached up to heav - en as the cross was raised, And

with His life He paid the price of praise. When praise de -

58
a tempo
mands a sac - ri - fice, I'll wor-ship e - ven then, Sur -
A Aadd9 A/C♯ E/D D E/F♯ F♯/A♯
f a tempo
62
ren - der-ing the dear - est things in life.
Bm B9sus Bm/A Bm/G♯ E/G♯ E(no 3rd)/F♯
66
And if de - vo - tion costs me all, He'll find me
And
C♯/E♯ F♯9sus F♯m F♯m/E

faith - ful to___ His call, When___ praise de - mands a sac - ri - fice. God hears the words of praise__ we lift. Yet I have found He's hon - ored more by what I'm
Yet I found that He is hon - ored,

willing to lay down. I'm willing to lay down. When praise demands a sacrifice, I'll worship even then, Surrendering the dearest things in life.

And if devotion costs me all, He'll find me faithful to His call, When praise demands a sacrifice.

And if devotion costs me all, He'll find me faithful to His

86

High and Exalted
Moments of Praise

Arr. by Tom Fettke

Majestic ♩ = ca. 76

A little faster ♩ = ca. 80

⑧ **"The Love of God"** *(Ken Bible and F.M.L. - Frederick M. Lehman)*

live,_____ and He is Lord,_____ Now crowned with heav - en's high-est

Copyright 1917, Renewed 1945 by Nazarene Publishing House. New text © 1992 by Pilot Point Music. All rights reserved.
Administered by Integrated Copyright Group, Inc., P.O. Box 24149, Nashville, TN 37202.

name; And there in Him, by love re-stored, With all cre-a-tion we'll pro-claim: "Worth-y the Lamb, the Great I Am, All glo-ry, pow'r and might." With joy we'll trace____ His bound-less grace____ In all its depth____ and height. O love of God,____ how rich and pure!____ How mea-sure-less____ and strong. It shall for -

ev - er-more en - dure_____ The saints' and an - gels' song._____

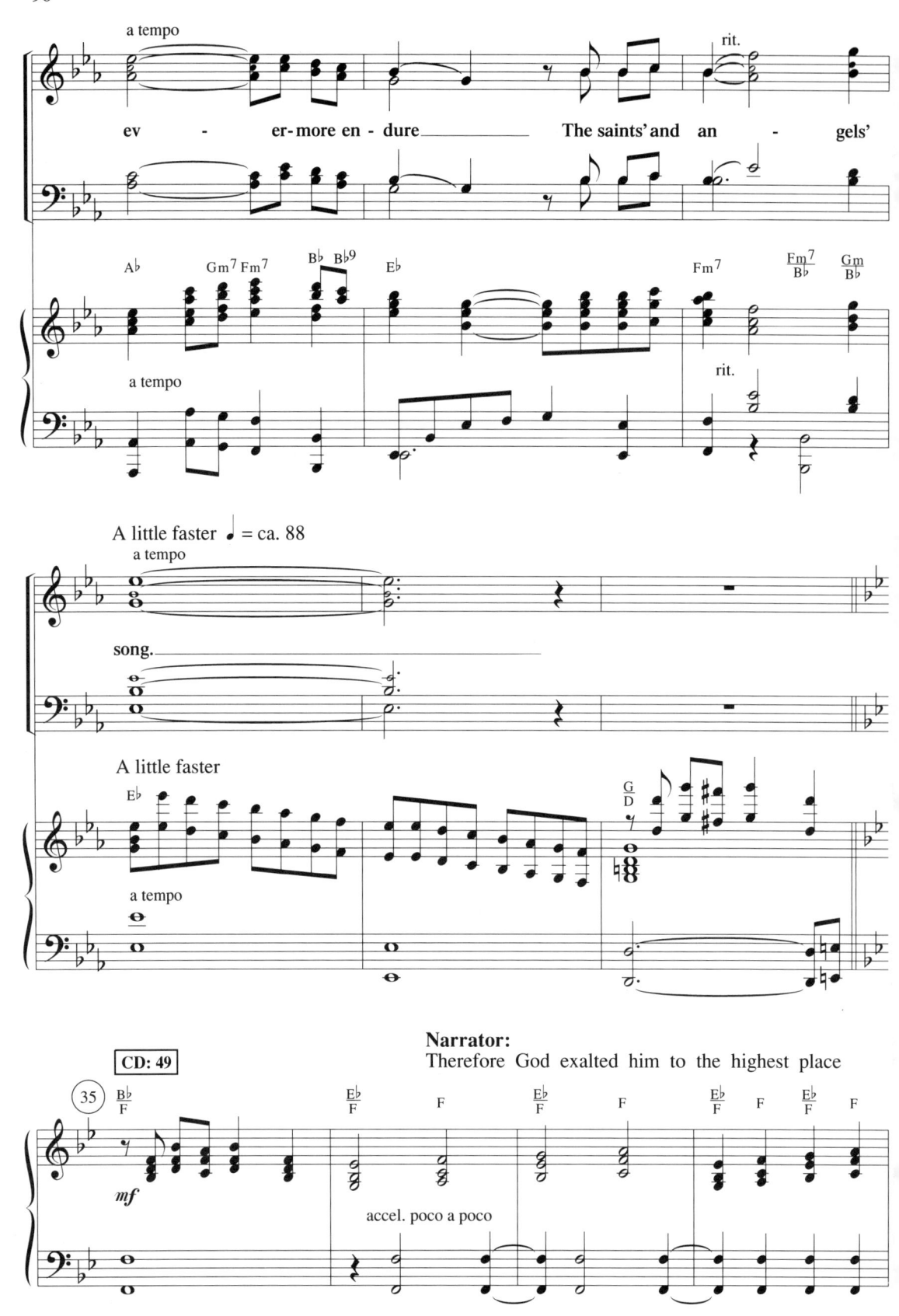

Narrator: Therefore God exalted him to the highest place and gave him the name that is above every name, that at the name of Jesus

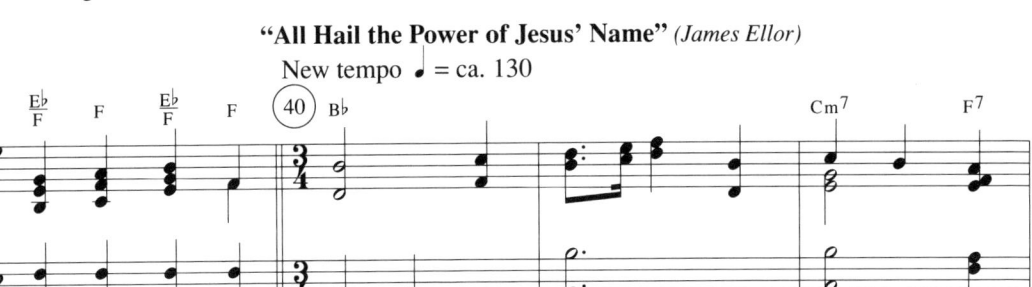

"All Hail the Power of Jesus' Name" *(James Ellor)*

New tempo ♩ = ca. 130

every knee should bow, in heaven and on earth and under the earth,

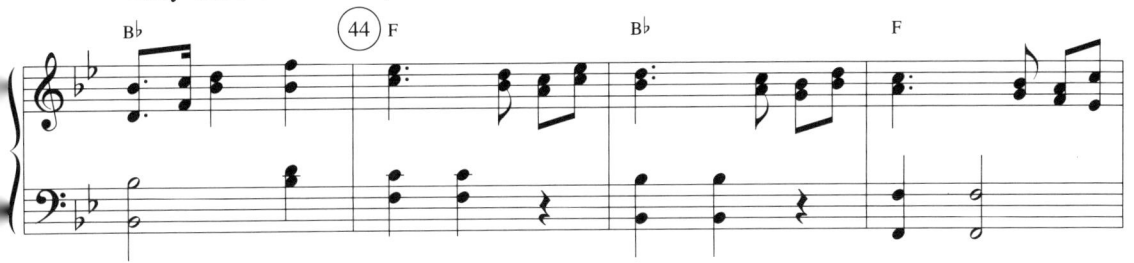

and every tongue confess that Jesus Christ is Lord,   to the glory of God the Father.
(Phil. 2: 9-11)

CD: 50

Unison **f**

Ex -

*"Exalt His Name Together" *(Jack Hayford)*

alt His name to-geth - er, the name of Je-sus laud; And mag-ni-fy the Sav - ior, the match-less Son of God. At His name dev-ils trem - ble and earth-ly king-doms fall; So

*© 1966 Gospel Publishing House. All rights reserved.

praise the name of Je - sus, the name high o - ver all.

Ladies unison (or solo) **Smoother**

Bow down and give Him rev - 'rence, this Je - sus glo - ri - fied, Who took our sins to

Cal-v'ry and in our place He died. But death could not con-tain Him; He smashed the gates of hell, So praise the name of Je-sus, His

con - q'ring pow - er tell. The

Stronger

morn - ing stars did praise Him be - fore all time be -

gan; An - gel - ic choirs wor - shipped at

97
birth this Son of Man. And through the end - less a - ges His
Div.
Am/G Am add9/F♯ Am/F♯ Dm/G Em/G F/G G
97 C
C/E Gsus/D C
3
101
name a - dored shall be; So praise the name of Je - sus Now
F Esus E/G♯ Am C/G F
101 C/E F E Am Am7
cresc.
105
and e - ter - nal - ly. So praise the name of Je - sus Now
Dm7 CM7/E F6 F6/G F/G C CM7 F
105 C/E C/D C Dm/B Dm/A E/G♯ Am Am/G

"He Is the Amen" (David Ritter)

A- men! A- men! The fin- al rev- e- la- tion. A- men! A- men!

119
He is the great A - men! He is the
Dm C/E F6 C/G E/G♯ Am 119 Dm C/E F
great A - men! He is the great A -
C/G E7/G♯ Am Dm C/E F6 1 Gsus G
men! He is the
C/G F/G Gsus

2
128
great
A - men!
2 Gsus
G
128 Csus
fff
He is the great
A -
C
C/B♭
F/A
Fm/A♭
G7sus
133
men!
133
N.C.
C